Made in United States
Orlando, FL
02 August 2025

63486556R00056